RITA CASTAGNA

Mantua
History and Art

EDIZIONI MORETTI

CONTENTS

Early History	3
The Bonacolsi Family	10
The Gonzaga Family	13
The Golden Age of the Gonzaga Family	15
Palazzo Ducale	29
Palazzo Te	51
The Decline	59
Maria Theresa and Mantua	61

Early History

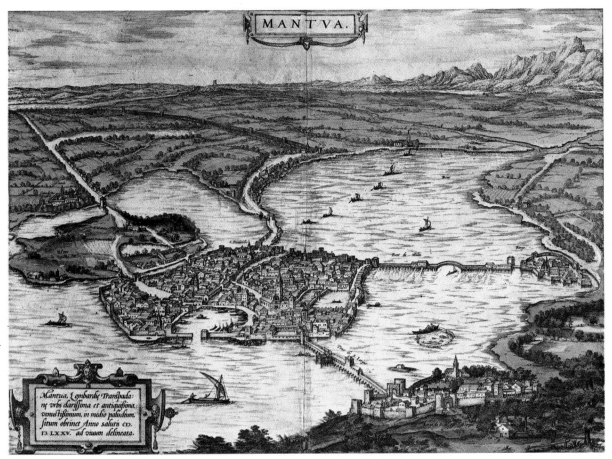

Dante tells us that the soothsayer Manto, after many years of wandering, decided to settle where the river Mincio, descending from the green mountain pastures, widens into a marshy lowland. Here she lived, practiced her magic and eventually died. Her followers and the few inhabitants of the area gathered in this spot, well protected by the surrounding marsh, and built their city over her grave. In her honour they called the city Mantua.

Surrounded as it is by three lakes which form a protective membrane of water, the city, even today, seems the result of some arcane magic. Dante's lines on the supposed origins of Mantua, though scarcely historical, merely add to the fasci-

nation of this city which, sheltered by the massive walls of its castle, has preserved the position and elegance of a small capital.

Another tradition has it that Mantua was founded by the Etruscans in the 6th century BC and that her name comes from the Etruscan god of the underworld, Mantus. However, this theory has never been definitely substantiated by archeologists.

Mantua came under Roman domination sometime between the first and second Punic Wars without however becoming an important urban centre.

Successive waves of invasion swept over the

3

(previous page)
*Map of the city in 1575.
Mantua, State Archives.*

*The Rotonda di San
Lorenzo, built probably
around 1082.*

(right)
*Palazzo del Podestà,
built in 1227 but
renovated in 1462.*

(below right)
*The bell-tower
of the Cathedral.*

city. First came the Visigoths, then the Huns and Lombards. The Byzantines conquered it for a brief period and then it passed to the Carolingians and then to the Emperor Berengarius.

Around 977 Mantua became part of the territory of the Canossa family. Documents show that in 1014 the urban centre extended into the present Piazza Sordello and its surroundings. The modest group of houses of no real artistic importance which constituted the city at this point were enriched by further building under the energetic rule of Matilda of Canossa who was called "the great Countess".

The only building extant from the age of Matilda is the Rotonda di San Lorenzo which was built, according to tradition, on the ruins of a pagan temple in 1082. Round in form, as its name implies, and with a matroneum (woman's gallery), the Rotonda is very similar to the church of San Tomé near Bergamo. Inside are traces of the early decorations and frescoes from the 12th and 13th centuries.

With the death of Matilda in 1115 began the period of the Commune. This was the period when intense rivalry between the city's most powerful families led to violent conflict; it was also marked by a notable expansion of the city itself. In 1198 the architect Alberto Pitentino changed the course of the Mincio river creating the lakes that encircle Mantua. Forming a natural moat these lakes provide both a superb defence and create that effect of a city rising from the water which is one of Mantua's greatest beauties.

Many Romanesque churches were constructed only to be demolished later and re-built with the style and dimensions that satisfied the limitless ambitions of the Gonzaga. Only a few bell-towers from this period are still standing; the most important and beautiful one is the solid and massive tower of the Cathedral. The building "boom" at the time of the Commune produced primarily civic buildings, those found between the Piazza delle Erbe and Piazza Broletto.

The Palazzo del Podestà was built in 1227 and is the impressive dividing line between the Piazza Broletto and the Piazza delle Erbe. In 1462 Gio-

vanni Antonio d'Arezzo carried out a Renaissance renovation on the palace which imposed an incongruous theatricality on the simple and solid Romanesque structure.

In a rectangular niche which dominates the Piazza Broletto is a charmingly unsophisticated statue of Virgil, the work of an unknown sculptor done at the time of the construction of the palace. Virgil, this greatest of Latin poets, is a sort of household god in the city of his birth.

At the end of the piazza is the great 13th-century Arengario, the double-arched loggia connecting the Palazzo Comunale with what was once Palazzo del Massaro. The dark vaulted ceiling of the Arcone, the connecting arch, evokes images of violence and suffering. One can still see huge rings suspended from the ribs of the ceiling. These were part of an infamous torture: the victim's hands were tied behind his back and then chained to the rings; then the poor wretch was lifted by means of a pulley until he hung in the air. A horrible punishment that was commuted to simple flogging for citizens who were under

Statue of Virgil, by an unknown 13th-century sculptor.

(right)
The outside staircase of the Sottoportico dei Lattonai.

(right)
Palazzo della Ragione in the Piazza delle Erbe, built in 1250.

age, for pregnant women or for those suffering from hernia.

The Sottoportico dei Lattonai with its outside stairway is situated in the narrow courtyard of the Palazzo del Podestà and leads to the spacious Piazza delle Erbe where the crenellated Palazzo della Ragione, built in 1250, joins the building. The entire "piano nobile" (the first floor of the building) is given over to the majestic hall where justice was dispensed. Traces of important Romanesque frescoes can be seen on the walls.

At the same period it was decided to enlarge the church and the convent of Santa Maria del Gradaro as the religious community of the Sisters of San Marco had increased considerably. Work began on the church in 1256 and continued until 1295 when a beautiful marble door, the work of the Veronese artists Giacomo and Ognabene Gratasoia was placed there. The church underwent various changes and alterations inside. It was suppressed in the late 18th century, turned into a military building and then it fell into ruins. Recent and intelligently planned work has restored

the church to its original form, a monument of both historic and artistic importance.

In the centre of the façade, surrounded by an elegant frame made of brick, is the great circular rose window which dates from the beginning of the 15th century. The inside of the church is divided into a nave and two aisles with pointed arches supported by brick columns. The dividing walls, on which traces of frescoes and decorations can be seen, separate the section of the choir designated for the members of the convent from that used by the laity.

The paintings and architectural designs on the walls of the aisles date from the renovation of the church in the 16th century. In the presbytery and the sacristy are remains of Byzantine frescoes dating from the late 13th century.

The façade of the church of Santa Maria del Gradaro, with the door built by Giacomo and Ognabene Gratasoia.

Interior of the church of Santa Maria del Gradaro.

The cloister of the convent of Santa Maria del Gradaro.

The Bonacolsi Family

Towards the end of the 13th century the internal political equilibrium was more precarious than ever and the tensions existing between the city's powerful families were strained to the breaking point. The government of the Commune was disintegrating and the moment of Pinamonte Bonacolsi was approaching. His undeniable gifts of courage and intelligence, plus the conspicuous family fortune, paved the way for the seizure of power on 4 July 1272.

The brief reign of the Bonacolsi left behind the impressive crenellated buildings which lined the two longer sides of the Piazza Sordello. The

The tower known as 'Torre della Gabbia' with, in the background, the Palazzo del Capitano.

palace next to the Voltone di San Pietro is alongside a tall tower built in the same period which is known as the Torre della Gabbia (Tower of the Cage). This name dates from the 16th century when Duke Guglielmo Gonzaga actually had an outdoor cage built here for prisoners.

To the right of the Cathedral the Palazzo del Capitano and the Magna Domus were built. Unchanged in their elegant proportions they formed the first nucleus of the Palazzo Ducale

Palazzo Bonacolsi in Piazza Sordello, built in the late 13th century.

where the Gonzaga lived in princely splendour for almost four centuries.

Also in the period of the Bonacolsi the first mendicant orders appeared in the city and, as they flourished, churches and convents were built for them in the Gothic style.

The church of San Francesco was built between 1303 and 1304 by an architect known to us only as Germano. Badly damaged by bombing in 1945 the entire complex, consisting also of the great convent and numerous cloisters, has been partially reconstructed and restored.

Inside, the church has a nave and two aisles. Plain and austere, the Franciscan church in Lombard-Gothic style is evocative of mystery and faith in its bareness, bareness relieved only by fragments of fresco decoration from various periods in its history. At the end of the right nave is the Cappella dei Signori or Gonzaga Chapel, at one time the burial place of the reigning family. It was frescoed in the 14th century with scenes from the life of Saint Louis of Toulouse attributed to Serafino de' Serafini. In the scene of the saint's

The church of San Francesco, built at the beginning of the 14th century.

(left)
The Death of St Louis, *attributed to Serafino de' Serafini, in the Cappella dei Signori.*

burial the founder of the house of Gonzaga, Luigi, is portrayed dressed in a white robe, his bowed head covered by a hood with precious embroidery.

The Bonacolsi rule was brief and ended in tragedy and bloodshed. In the fierce struggle for power the descendants of Pinamonte Bonacolsi underestimated the political astuteness, the ability, the ambition and the willingness to compromise of the family who turned Mantua into one of the most admired capitals of Europe: the Gonzaga.

The Gonzaga Family

The Expulsion of the Bonacolsi, *by Domenico Morone.*

Notwithstanding the considerable effort of genealogists to discover an aristocratic strain, the fact remains that the Gonzaga were of peasant origin and in the 12th century lived under the protection of the Monastery of San Benedetto in Polirone. The Monastery, founded by the Canossa, received many donations from the rich and devout and from the Canossa family themselves. Rich in land the monastery broke up its property into small holdings which were rented or even given to those who promised to cultivate the land or to those whom the monks befriended. Beginning in a small way the Gonzaga were thus able to accumulate considerable rural property. They moved to the city where, early in the 13th century, after previous sporadic appearances in political life, they began to assume a decisive role in the city's development.

Ambition and wealth increased in equal measure and in 1328 Luigi, head of the house of Gonzaga, prepared and carried out a spectacular takeover. A dramatic *coup d'état* played out against a backdrop of the city's squares and illuminated by moonlight on a humid August night. Cangrande della Scala (the lord of neighbouring Verona), who had hopes of conquering Mantua for himself, was generous in sending troops who entered the city silently from the Porta Mulina.

The last of the Bonacolsi, Rinaldo called "il Passerino" slept soundly in one of the cool, high-ceilinged rooms of his palace. All of his followers were asleep and were awakened by shouting and the sound of running men. Rinaldo rushed out of his palace, mounted his horse and raced towards the Piazza delle Erbe. He was severely wounded by the sword of one of the conspirators and his horse brought him back to the safety of his palace. In the desperate attempt to dismount and to open the great doors of his palace that the servants had closed, Bonacolsi, already weak from loss of blood, slipped and struck his head against the doors; he fell to the ground and died, his body sprawled across the threshold of his palace.

13

The Castello di San Giorgio.

The uprising ended in a triumph for the Gonzaga family. Luigi, the mastermind of the plot, entered the Cathedral amidst waving banners, black stripes on gold background, and offered the traditional *Te Deum* of thanks. The scene of *The Expulsion of the Bonacolsi* was painted many years later (1494) by Domenico Morone. This great canvas, as colourful and full of movement as a ballet, still hangs in the Palazzo Ducale.

Busy consolidating their position, Luigi and his immediate successors paid little attention to building. Early in the Gonzaga rule only slight alterations to the Magna Domus and the Palazzo del Capitano were carried out. It was only towards the end of the 13th century that a descendant of Luigi's, Francesco I, had the Casa Giocosa built, probably to get away from his sickly, nagging wife, Agnese Visconti, and to provide himself with a place for his extra-marital adventures. The Casa Giocosa was next to the Magna Domus; at the end of the 16th century it was demolished to make way for a superb garden created for Duke Guglielmo.

Meanwhile a new city wall was built with five great gates: San Giorgio, Cerese, Pusterla, Pradella and Mulina. The considerably expanded urban centre was divided into four quarters: Santo Stefano, San Giacomo, San Martino and San Leonardo. Inside the fortified circle the architect Bartolino da Novara built, towards the end of the 14th century, the Castello di San Giorgio whose battlements rise solid and sure in defence of the city. At this same time the present Piazza Sordello was built by demolishing some of the buildings that were still standing from the reign of the Bonacolsi family. Thus a framework was created for the future splendour of the Gonzaga Dukes. Francesco I had a passion for building as did many other members of the Gonzaga family. He commissioned the Venetian brothers Jacomello and Pier Paolo dalle Masegne to renovate the Romanesque Cathedral giving it a new Gothic façade. This reconstruction is visible in its entirety today only in the painting *The Expulsion of the Bonacolsi*. The right side of the Cathedral itself with its cusps and pinnacles is the only part of this Gothic structure still standing.

The Golden Age of the Gonzaga Family

Pisanello: Medal with the portrait of Cecilia Gonzaga, daughter of Gianfrancesco, Marquis of Mantua. Paris, Bibliothèque Nationale.

Captains of the People with dictatorial powers, the lords of Mantua were a strange blend of farmers and soldiers. Lengthy negotiations with the German Emperor Sigismond Hohenzollern, who habitually squeezed money from families seeking aristocratic titles, finally brought the title of Marquis to Gianfrancesco Gonzaga in 1433. His Imperial Majesty demanded exorbitant terms for the marquisate: twelve thousand gold florins, an enormous sum for those days. As a bonus (and further proof of the size of the payment), Sigismond gave his niece Barbara of Brandenburg as a wife to Gianfrancesco's son Ludovico and even permitted the Gonzaga to quarter the imperial eagles on their coat-of-arms.

Gianfrancesco was the prime mover in the International Gothic period in Mantua, although in him the construction mania was less pronounced and this period produced no exceptional buildings.

Between 1413 and 1414 the Bell-tower of the church of Sant'Andrea was built. In 1423 the Casa Giocosa, built for Francesco I's escapades, was turned into the seat of the Humanist academy of

Vittorino da Feltre, tutor of the Marquis's sons.

The artistic world of Gianfrancesco, which centred round the International Gothic style, had as its greatest exponent not an architect but a painter, Pisanello, who began working at the court of the Gonzaga about 1425. He created famous and beautiful medals of Vittorino da Feltre, Cecilia, Gianfrancesco and Ludovico Gonzaga and around 1444, shortly before his patron's death, he was commissioned to fresco a room in the Corte Vecchia. The work remained unfinished and disappeared until Professor Giovanni Paccagnini rediscovered it in 1969. The Pisanello cycle of paintings will be discussed in detail in the chapter on the Palazzo Ducale.

A disciple of Vittorino da Feltre, the intellectual Ludovico II, succeeded Gianfrancesco. He surrounded himself with Humanist philosophers, men

of letters and artists such as Leon Battista Alberti, Mantegna and Luca Fancelli. Under his efficient rule Mantua entered a period of renovation and reconstruction without altering its essential medieval character.

The house of the merchant Giovanni Boniforte (1455), a delicate and elegant mixture of oriental and Venetian styles, was one of the last International Gothic buildings in the city.

During his frequent stays in Mantua Leon Battista Alberti planned and designed the churches of San Sebastiano (1460) and Sant'Andrea (1472). The execution of his plans was entrusted to Luca Fancelli, the leading architect at the court of Ludovico II.

Today San Sebastiano is a war memorial. Its spacious interior, in the form of a Greek cross, is covered by a large cross-vault with four large niches. The simple and severe façade is decorated only with five arches placed on two levels. A lamentable restoration in 1927 ruined its geometric perfection by closing off two entrances to the crypt with a bulky, heavy staircase.

Meanwhile, Ludovico II decided to move from the Corte Vecchia into the Castello di San Giorgio.

The house of the merchant.
Giovanni Boniforte da Concorezzo.

(left)
The bell-tower of the church of Sant'Andrea.

(right)
The façade of the church of San Sebastiano.

(below)
Detail of cherubs with the coat-of-arms of the Gonzaga, from the façade of San Sebastiano.

Courtyard of the Castello di San Giorgio (1472), by Luca Fancelli.

(right) Interior of the church of Sant'Andrea.

(below left) The façade of the church of Sant'Andrea, constructed by Luca Fancelli from a design by Leon Battista Alberti.

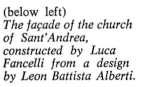

He ordered Luca Fancelli and Andrea Mantegna to transform the castle into a comfortable and luxurious residence without in any way altering its forbidding appearance of a fortress. Luca Fancelli also worked on the construction of the courtyard of the castle which was surrounded by an elegant two winged portico designed by Andrea Mantegna.

In the same year work was begun on the church of Sant'Andrea; the proportions and grandness of this church were visible signs of the boundless ambitions of the Gonzaga. Ludovico II finally obtained permission from Pope Sixtus IV to demolish the existing Gothic church which by then seemed too simple and out of date. Luca Fancelli was given the difficult job of carrying out Alberti's plans and projects. Work continued intermittently throughout several centuries and was not entirely completed until the 18th century with the creation of the overblown Baroque cupola of Filippo Juvara.

Setting aside the conventional plans for medieval architecture Alberti envisaged a singularly original façade using motifs from Roman triumphal arches. The great space inside is in the form of a Latin cross, with a transept covered by the 18th-century dome. In the first chapel on the left on entering the church is a simple marble slab marking the burial place of Andrea Mantegna who died in

Mantua in 1506. In the same chapel is a bust of the great artist which is the work of Gian Marco Cavalli, the official engraver of the Mint. Cavalli has so brilliantly portrayed the rugged, lined face of the artist that the work is sometimes attributed to Mantegna himself and Cavalli is credited only with the execution of the master's design.

In the crypt, which was designed by Anton Maria Viani at the end of the 16th century, is the reliquary containing the blood of Christ which, according to legend, was brought to Mantua by Longinus, the Roman soldier who thrust his spear into Christ's side. This precious testament of Christ's martyrdom is contained in a pair of golden vases created by the Milanese goldsmith Giovanni Bellezza in the 19th century. Their design is based on the original vases by Cellini, commissioned by Isabella d'Este, stolen by the Austrians in 1848.

Under the direction of the indefatigable Luca Fancelli, work began in 1473 on the Torre dell'Orologio (the Clock Tower) between Palazzo della Ragione and the Rotonda di San Lorenzo. The great clock was conceived by Bartolomeo Man-

(left)
Interior of the dome of Sant'Andrea.

(below left)
*Bust of Andrea Mantegna,
by Gian Marco Cavalli.*

*The Torre dell'orologio
(Clock Tower) and the Rotonda
di San Lorenzo.*

fredi, astronomer, mathematician, clock-maker and astrologer of the court. "The great invention", as it was justifiably called, not only told the time of day but provided a horoscope and also told the Mantuans the proper days in which to prune plants, take medecine, go to the doctor, start on trips or make clothes. The complex mechanism of Master Bartolomeo's masterpiece was already in need of serious repair in 1547. Valiant efforts were made throughout the centuries to repair it completely but without success. Today this exceptional mechanism only manages to show the correct time of day.

The terrible plague which attacked Mantua in 1478 carried off Ludovico II in spite of the fact that he had fled to his villa in Goito to escape contagion. Of the son who inherited the difficult position of following such an intelligent and efficient ruler little is known. Federico I governed only six years and is known primarily for his appreciation of art and literature. A contemporary chronicler, Schivenoglia, called him "that polite and pleasant hunchback". In fact he was afflicted with the Gonzaga hump probably brought into the family by his grandmother, Paola Malatesta. He loved elegance and luxury and was responsible for the construction of the impressive Domus Nova, begun by Luca Fancelli around 1480. This building, a part of the Palazzo Ducale complex, remained unfinished because of Federico's death in 1484.

The cylindrical courtyard in Mantegna's house.

(right)
Detail of Francesco II Gonzaga from the Madonna of Victory *by Andrea Mantegna, now in the Louvre in Paris.*

Sometime between 1476 and 1496 Andrea Mantegna's house was built near the church of San Sebastiano: a solid construction enclosing a cylindrical courtyard. Whether Mantegna actually designed his own house is a controversial question as there are no documents to support this theory. However, the similarities with the round ceiling oculus in the square Camera degli Sposi lend credence to the belief that Mantegna in some way had a part in the construction of the house in which he lived.

A famous painting of Mantegna's, the *Madonna of Victory* now in the Louvre, shows us the features of the fourth Marquis, Francesco II. The kneeling warrior is shown in profile, his well formed body in splendid armour; full red lips, high cheekbones accentuated by a curly black beard, the Marquis possessed the attraction of virility and sensuality rather than traditional male

beauty. He was not literary like his grandfather but loved horses, tournaments and blood sports. He had a particular propensity for the sensual and earthy pleasures of life. The biographer Coniglio says of him in his book on the Gonzaga: "he read the lives of the saints in the same spirit in which he read the obscenities that the jurist Floriano Dolfo wrote for him safe in the knowledge that they would be properly appreciated". Completely different from Francesco was his celebrated wife, Isabella d'Este. Intelligent, ambitious and cultivated, Isabella made her life into a masterpiece of aesthetic perfection, literary, artistic and musical. Much has been written about her as one of the great figures of the Renaissance and, truthfully, she needs far more space than can be given to her here. This inimitable woman gave particular and passionate attention to her collection of *objets d'art* and paintings which she assembled in her rooms in the castle and, after her widowhood, in the Corte Vecchia of the Palazzo Ducale.

Under the influence of Isabella the court of Mantua became one of the most brilliant in all Italy. It was this atmosphere of Humanism that formed Federico II, the adored son of Isabella and Francesco. The future lord of Mantua spent two years as a hostage in the luxurious papal court of Julius II in Rome and there his artistic taste became very Roman. In 1519 his father died of syphilis and Federico II came to power at the age of nineteen; almost immediately he began negotiations to bring Raphael's favorite pupil, Giulio Pippi, known to us as Giulio Romano, to Mantua. Thanks to the good offices of Baldassarre Castiglione, author of *The Courtier* and the Gonzaga's ambassador to Rome, Giulio arrived in Mantua in 1524 and quickly proved himself the perfect artist for the ambitious Marquis. Giving free reign to his fondness for "the fantastic and the rhetorical", Giulio created a fabulous palace for Federico and imposed an artistic dictatorship on the city much as Andrea Mantegna had done in his own way forty years earlier. He was an ingenious and imaginative artist and renovated the city giving it the overall artistic style that it still possesses. Within the space of a few years he created the Palazzo Te, the Palazzina della Paleologa, the Appartamento di Troia and the Palazzina Rustica in the Palazzo Ducale. Federico II, always in quest of new titles and honours, received the Emperor Charles V in his renovated capital in 1530. The Emperor elevated the Gonzaga to the rank of Dukes. The following year Federico's rather unattractive wife, Margherita Paleologo, brought him Monferrato as part of her dowry.

Giulio Romano's intense artistic activity continued without let-up and the Macello (slaughter house)

The house of Giulio Romano.

(above)
The Pescherie, from a project by Giulio Romano.

(right)
Interior of the Cathedral.

was also built at this time. This building of Giulio's along the canal had two adjacent porticoes called the "Pescherie". The Macello itself was destroyed in the 19th century but the Pescherie are still standing. Towards the end of his life Giulio built his own house which was finished sometime after 1538. The façade of Giulio's house, a row of rusticated arches resting on a strong and solid base, was altered in the 19th century during a restoration carried out by Paolo Pozzo.

The Hunting Lodge of Bosco
della Fontana, near Marmirolo.

(right)
The church of Sant'Orsola.

(far right)
The church of San Maurizio.

(below right)
The Palazzo Gonzaga di
Vescovato, today the Palace
of Justice.

Federico II passed the last years of his short life in peaceful enjoyment of the treasures and beauties of his dukedom. The death of his mother Isabella in 1539 did little to upset his tranquillity. But the following year a particularly virulent attack of the disease from which he suffered (probably congenital syphilis) killed him. He was only forty years old when he died in his villa at Marmirolo surrounded by the splendid things he loved. His brother Cardinal Ercole became Regent because of the extreme youth of his son, the new Duke Francesco III. The pagan atmosphere of Federico's reign was followed by a climate of austerity. The adaptable Giulio Romano quickly learned to follow the new line of the court. During this intermediate period of the Cardinal's regency, Giulio presented his project for the restoration of the inside of the Cathedral which had been destroyed by fire in 1545. The Cathedral was thus given its present appearance without destroying the existing Gothic structure. The nave is lined with parallel lines of Corinthian columns topped by a continuous frieze with a decoration of reliefs; above this are alternating windows and niches. The ceiling is coffered, like the ceilings of the outer aisles. The inner aisles are barrel-vaulted.

Giulio's designs are derived from Early Christian basilicas in Rome but are heightened by his ever lively inventiveness. The multiplicity of decoration keeps the visitor from getting a general or overall view of the church, instead it seems that the building has been broken into thousands of kaleidoscopic fragments. Giulio lived to supervise only part of his project; the work was finished by Giovan Battista Bertani in a rather cold and academic manner.

Death came to Giulio in November 1546 and the entire court mourned the loss of this dynamic and brilliant artist to the point that Cardinal Ercole wrote to his brother Ferrante: "We have lost our Giulio Romano and it seems that we have lost our right hand."

The reign of Francesco III was extremely brief and in 1550 the dukedom passed into the hands of Guglielmo. The new Duke was a misanthropic bigot, his body deformed by the hereditary hump. He accumulated large sums of money and his ambition led him to marry one of the Austrian Emperor's daughters, Eleonora, a huge woman with bulging eyes.

The Mantuan Giovan Battista Bertani was named successor to Giulio Romano as artistic Superintendent of Works of the duchy. His duties were confined primarily to the upkeep and enlargement of already existing properties.

With the accession of Guglielmo's son, Vincenzo I, came the last great flowering of Mantuan art and culture. Handsome, loving, gregarious, the new

prince was the very opposite of his father. A complex man with a predilection for getting into trouble, Vincenzo was involved in duels, amatory scandals and a series of Boccaccio-like adventures. It is a mistake to think of him merely as a womaniser or a voluptuary dedicated only to sensual pleasure and luxury. Above all he was an able and astute diplomat who managed to keep peace in the warlike province of Monferrato. He also paid great attention to the glorification of his capital and his duchy which grew ever richer and more splendid under his rule. An avid collector, intelligent patron of the arts and passionate music lover he called to his court famous artists such as Rubens, Monteverdi, Jacopo Peri and il Guarino. Anton Maria Viani took up the demanding position of court architect under Vincenzo I and built sumptuous residences throughout the realm and many civil and religious buildings in the city itself. Viani completed the hunting lodge of Bosco della Fontana near Marmirolo, one of the many residences in the dukedom devoted to the pursuit of pleasure.

He designed the monastery and the church of Sant'Orsola (1603) with its octagonal plan. He was also responsible for the church of San Maurizio (1604). Around 1614 the court architect planned the splendid Palazzo dei Gonzaga di Vescovato. This building is now the Palace of Justice. Vincenzo I died in 1612 and with his

The villa La Favorita. built by Nicolò Sebregondi between 1616 and 1624.

passing ended the Gonzaga's period of glory.

The death of this remarkable man left debts and family problems that were overwhelming for his successors who had inherited none of the genius or vitality of their father. Francesco IV left behind neither lasting traces of his rule nor a male heir as a direct successor. He was succeeded by his brother, Ferdinando, who had to resign from the College of Cardinals in order to take over the government of Mantua. Ferdinando was also interested in art and literature and called to the court the young Roman painter Domenico Fetti as well as Saraceni, Baglione and Albani who were commissioned to decorate the sumptuous villa called La Favorita. Years before the Bourbons created Versailles, Ferdinando had the idea of moving the seat of government away from the city to create a distinct division between his court and the city of his subjects. To this end he had La Favorita built on the far side of the middle lake. The architect was Nicolò Sebregondi who worked on the project from 1616 to 1624. Only a grandiose ruin remains today of this once impressive and luxurious residence: fire, war, plunder and time have destroyed the original.

The brief reign of Ferdinando gave only a temporary respite to the downward course of the family and of Mantua itself. Vincenzo II succeeded his brother as once again there was no direct heir. He quickly found himself in political and financial difficulties that he was unable to solve. An inept politician who cared only for his creature comforts and the pursuit of pleasure, Vincenzo II found himself in 1630 overcome by debts. He was forced to sell many of the family paintings to Charles I of England. The price paid for this fabulous collection was far short of its actual market value. Among the masterpieces sold to Charles I were: Titian's *Concert, Deposition* and the lost *Portraits of the Caesars*; allegorical canvases by Correggio; the *Triumphs* of Mantegna and a portrait by Giovanni Bellini. The art dealer Daniel Nys, who acted as intermediary in this sale, wrote to Lord Dorchester in February 1629 that Vincenzo had sold the paintings "... for 68,000 scudi to the surprise of all Italy and the disgust of the people of Mantua."

The problems increased and the weak willed Vincenzo was unable to cope with them. He was trapped in an unhappy and sterile marriage and at his death the duchy passed to Carlo Rethel Gonzaga Nevers, a French princeling belonging to a cadet branch of the family.

Palazzo Ducale

Palazzo del Capitano, seen from the bell-tower of the Cathedral.

The magnificent group of buildings that make up the Palazzo Ducale must be studied as an architectural unit distinct from the city, as the palace is in fact an autonomous urban centre. And such it has been from the height of Gonzaga power. It covered at one time an area of 34,000 square metres and extended from the Piazza Sordello eastwards to the lower lake.

The construction of this vast palace took place over many years beginning in the 14th and ending in the 17th century. Based on the 13th-century buildings of the Bonacolsi, the Magna Domus and the Palazzo del Capitano alongside the Piazza Sordello, the different structures were created around seven large light-filled gardens and eight internal courtyards. The great complex, fascinating in its variety of architectural styles, was united in the 16th century by a network of corridors and covered passageways that linked one building to

The corridor along the façade with International Gothic decorative motifs.

Pisanello's fresco cycle was re-discovered in 1969 by Professor Paccagnini: it is one of the most spectacular examples of International-Gothic art. The frescoes illustrate scenes from chivalric romances of Brittany.
Detail of a knight.

another. The construction and decoration of this fabulous palace was entrusted to famous artists such as: Pisanello, Mantegna, Fancelli, Lorenzo Leonbruno, Costa il Vecchio, Giulio Romano, Correggio, Titian, Tintoretto, Bertani, Viani, Rubens, Fetti and Daniel van Dyck. Symbol of the power, wealth and ambition of the Gonzaga family, the Palazzo Ducale was at once many things—a self-contained city, a fortress, a luxurious residence and a pivot for the entire political and civic life of the city.

After the 1328 takeover the new lords soon found the existing buildings insufficient for their needs. The first, rather modest addition, was built behind the Palazzo del Capitano around the end of the 14th century.

The long corridor along the façade, once divided into interlinking rooms, boasts a lavish decoration of heraldic motifs in the International Gothic style. The spirit of courtly chivalry, the guiding force of the Middle Ages, is displayed in shields, mottoes, geometric decoration and elaborate floral motifs. The large rooms off the corridor were transformed by Viani at the end of the 16th century into airy reception halls with wooden ceilings decorated with cherubs, mottoes and coats-of-arms of the Gonzaga.

Important frescoes dating from early Gonzaga rule were re-discovered at the beginning of this century. When the existing 16th-century decoration in the chapel was removed, a *Crucifixion* (unfortunately with its left side missing) and the figures of two saints were revealed. Arcangeli, the art historian, suggests that these might well be the work of Jacopino de' Bavosi, one of the 14th-century painters of northern Italy whose style might best be described as harshly realistic.

Francesco I was the first Gonzaga to take an interest in the architectural development of the palace. Under his auspices that superb example of military architecture, the Castello di San Giorgio, was built, as was the now vanished Casa Giocosa, prototype of the many country residences that the lords of Mantua built throughout the province.

With Marquis Gianfrancesco the splendid season of International Gothic began. He was away from Mantua a great deal (he often fought with his troops as a sort of aristocratic mercenary captain), and his primary concern was the aggrandisement of the existing palace rather than creating new buildings. His particular world was immortalised by one of the greatest exponents of International Gothic, Pisanello, "... this most subtle analyst of the world of chivalry and courtly manners, whose work is like a diary of a great nobleman who has lived always within this most cultivated and elegant world." During his frequent visits to Mantua, this Veronese painter frescoed one of the great halls of the Gonzaga palace. Letters to Federico I mention-

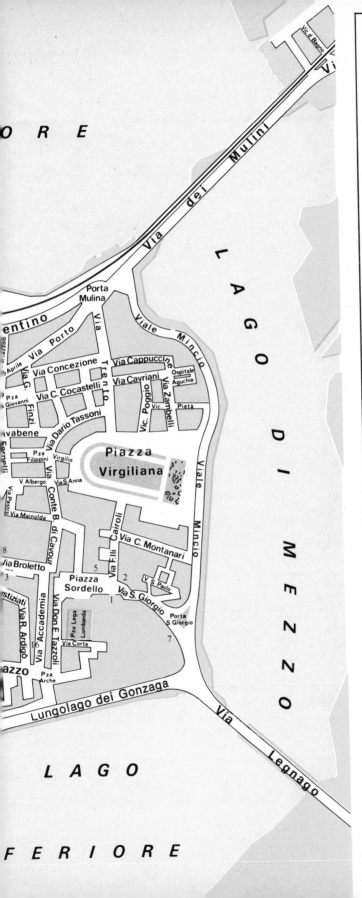

Mantova

1. Palazzo Ducale

2. Duomo

3. Piazza delle Erbe:
   Palazzo della Ragione;
   Torre dell'Orologio,
   Rotonda di San Lorenzo,
   Casa del mercante

4. Santa Maria del Gradaro

5. Palazzo Bonacolsi

6. San Francesco

7. Castello di San Giorgio

8. Sant'Andrea

9. San Sebastiano

10. Casa del Mantegna

11. Casa di Giulio Romano

12. Sant'Orsola

13. San Maurizio

14. Palazzo di Giustizia

15. Palazzo Te

16. Palazzo dell'Accademia

17. Palazzo D'Arco

18. Teatro Sociale

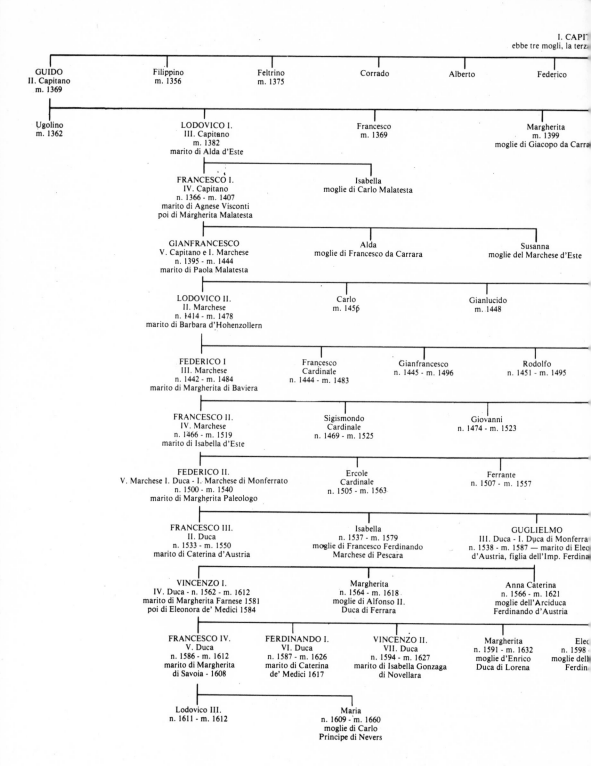

I Gonza[ga]

GUIDO
II. Capitano
m. 1369

Filippino
m. 1356

Feltrino
m. 1375

Corrado

Alberto

Federico

Ugolino
m. 1362

LODOVICO I.
III. Capitano
m. 1382
marito di Alda d'Este

Francesco
m. 1369

Margherita
m. 1399
moglie di Giacopo da Carra[ra]

FRANCESCO I.
IV. Capitano
n. 1366 - m. 1407
marito di Agnese Visconti
poi di Margherita Malatesta

Isabella
moglie di Carlo Malatesta

GIANFRANCESCO
V. Capitano e I. Marchese
n. 1395 - m. 1444
marito di Paola Malatesta

Alda
moglie di Francesco da Carrara

Susanna
moglie del Marchese d'Este

LODOVICO II.
II. Marchese
n. 1414 - m. 1478
marito di Barbara d'Hohenzollern

Carlo
m. 1456

Gianlucido
m. 1448

FEDERICO I
III. Marchese
n. 1442 - m. 1484
marito di Margherita di Baviera

Francesco
Cardinale
n. 1444 - m. 1483

Gianfrancesco
n. 1445 - m. 1496

Rodolfo
n. 1451 - m. 1495

FRANCESCO II.
IV. Marchese
n. 1466 - m. 1519
marito di Isabella d'Este

Sigismondo
Cardinale
n. 1469 - m. 1525

Giovanni
n. 1474 - m. 1523

FEDERICO II.
V. Marchese I. Duca - I. Marchese di Monferrato
n. 1500 - m. 1540
marito di Margherita Paleologo

Ercole
Cardinale
n. 1505 - m. 1563

Ferrante
n. 1507 - m. 1557

FRANCESCO III.
II. Duca
n. 1533 - m. 1550
marito di Caterina d'Austria

Isabella
n. 1537 - m. 1579
moglie di Francesco Ferdinando
Marchese di Pescara

GUGLIELMO
III. Duca - I. Duca di Monferra[to]
n. 1538 - m. 1587 — marito di Eleo[nora]
d'Austria, figlia dell'Imp. Ferdina[ndo]

VINCENZO I.
IV. Duca - n. 1562 - m. 1612
marito di Margherita Farnese 1581
poi di Eleonora de' Medici 1584

Margherita
n. 1564 - m. 1618
moglie di Alfonso II.
Duca di Ferrara

Anna Caterina
n. 1566 - m. 1621
moglie dell'Arciduca
Ferdinando d'Austria

FRANCESCO IV.
V. Duca
n. 1586 - m. 1612
marito di Margherita
di Savoia - 1608

FERDINANDO I.
VI. Duca
n. 1587 - m. 1626
marito di Caterina
de' Medici 1617

VINCENZO II.
VII. Duca
n. 1594 - m. 1627
marito di Isabella Gonzaga
di Novellara

Margherita
n. 1591 - m. 1632
moglie d'Enrico
Duca di Lorena

Eleo[nora]
n. 1598
moglie dell[a]
Ferdin[ando]

Lodovico III.
n. 1611 - m. 1612

Maria
n. 1609 - m. 1660
moglie di Carlo
Principe di Nevers

Mantova

8 — m. 1360
Malaspina sposata nel 1340

| one 413 | Giacomo | Giovanni | Marco | Tomasina moglie di Guglielmo di Castelbarco | Lisina moglie di Niccolò Fieschi | Domitilla moglie di Alidosio da Imola |

Tomasina
moglie di Azzone da Correggio

Beatrice
moglie di Niccolò d'Este

Elena

ro

Cecilia
m. 1451

Margherita
m. 1440
moglie di Leonello
Marchese di Ferrara

ovico
otario
m. 1511

Susanna
n. 1447 - m. 1481

Dorotea
n. 1449 - m. 1469

Cecilia
m. 1451

Barbara
n. 1455 - m. 1503

Paola
moglie di Leonardo
Conte di Gorizia

ra
03
Gilberto
ntpensier

Maddalena
m. 1490
moglie di Giovanni Sforza

Elisabetta
moglie di Guidôbaldo
Duca d'Urbino

eonora
4 - m. 1570
rancesco Maria
di Urbino

Ippolita
m. 1570

Paola
m. 1569

Lodovico
Duca di Nevers
n. 1539 - m. 1595
marito di Enrica di Clèves

Federico
Cardinale
n. 1541 - m. 1565

Luigia

Anna

CARLO DI NEVERS
VIII. Duca
n. 1580 - m. 1637
marito di Caterina di Lorena

Caterina
n. 1568
moglie d'Enrico d'Orléans

Enrichetta
moglie del Duca Du Maine

Carlo
Principe di Nevers
n. 1609 - m. 1631
marito di Maria Gonzaga
figlia di Francesco IV.
V. Duca

Francesco
m. 1622

Ferdinando
n. 1612 - m. 1632

Maria Luigia
m. 1666
moglie di Wladislao
e poi di Giancasimiro
ambi Re di Polonia

Anna
m. 1634
moglie di Odoardo
Conte Palatino

Benedetta

CARLO II.
IX Duca
n. 1629 - m. 1665
arito di Isabella Clara d'Austria - 1649

Eleonora
n. 1628 - m. 1686
moglie dell'Imperatore
Ferdinando III.

FERDINANDO CARLO
X. DUCA
n. 1652 - m. 1708
di Anna Isabella Gonzaga di Guastalla m. 1703
4 di Susanna Enrichetta di Lorena Elbeuf m. 1710

L A G

S U P E R

da Dosso del Corso

Belgioioso

Pompilio

Via Ciro Menotti

Cremona

Viale Monsignor Luigi Martini

Viale Dicembre

Viale

Via

Stazione F.F.S.S.

Viale T. Nuvolari

Viale G. Galilei

Viale

Vittorio Alfieri

Vle L. Da Vinci

Ple Michelangelo

Largo Petrarca

Vle Manzoni

Cremona

Lgo di Porta Pradella

Via S. Bettinelli

P. Dori E. Leoni

Via Alberto

Viale

Fiume

Viale

Viale

Viale

Oslavia

Pza Alcide De Gasperi

Vle Ortigara

Viale Sabotino

Viale Asiago

Corso

Viale Hermada

Fiume

V. Belfiore

V Solferino e S.Martino

Via S.Francesco d'Assisi

6

V.Sca

Viale

Viale A. Parilla

Vle G. E. Gobio

Gorizia

Viale

Viale Podgora

Viale Piave

Conciliazione

Vic. Montanara e Curtatone

V. Pero

Via Giosuè Carducci

Corso Vittorio Emanuele

Speri

V. Bonomi

V.Corrado

Via Maironi

Via Fil

12

Via Gio

Viale Montenero

Vle Luigi Vaschi

Vle d. Partigiani

Piazzale

Antonio

Gramsci

Vle Gen. Tellera

Via L. Fancelli

Via Enrico Dugoni

della

Via

V. Canal

V. Tito

A.M. Viani

V.A.Mario

Cavallotti

C.so di Libertà

C.so Umberto I

Pza T Folengo

V. Ippolit

18

Viale Brig. Mantova

Boschetti

Vle Bligny

Viale

Vle d. Chiesa

Via Fratelli Grioli

Pza G Bazzani

Giovanni

13'

A.M. Viani

Pza 80

Eccid

Via G. de' Cani

Chiassi

Via Roma

Pza Marcor

Viale Montello

Viale Monte Grappa

Vle d. Rimembranza

14

11

Via C. Poma

Via S. Crispino

13

Bden Fanteria

Spadaccio

Pza Martiri di Belfiore

Cso B Grazzi

Cso Don Bosco

Primaticcio

15

P.le Vittorio Veneto

Largo 24 Maggio

9

10

Via G. Acerbi

Via Principe Amedeo

Via Mazzini

Via 20 Settembre Matteotti

V Pescheria

RIO

Orefici

Vic. Forno

Filippo Corridoni

Viale Te

Viale Te

Platina

Via Gian

Battista

Visi

Federico

G.B. Fiera

Via D. Semeghini

Vle Lemburgno

Amedeo

Piazzale Monferrato

Cadioli

Via F Tonelli

Bonoris

Parma

Via degli Osanna

possevino

P.le Vittorio Veneto

Viale Te

Porta Pusteria

Viale Porta

Viale Risorgimento

Viale Isonzo

IPPODROMO

CAMPO SPORTIVO

Via N. Sauro

Via G. Rippa

Via V. Da Feltre

Via Valsesia

Via Attilio Mori

Giulio

Romano

Via

Via Isabella d'Este

Via G. Gonzaga

V.S. Egidio

V. Lorenzo

Pietro

Frattini

V.

Garibaldi

Corso Giuseppe Garibaldi

Piazza dei Mille

Via G. Benzoni

Gandolfo

V.Fl Elisi

Madonna

Via Massari

V.Flli Bronzetti

Via Trieste

Via Cardone

Via G. Govi

Via

Via Fondamenta

Piazza Anconetta

Via Argine

Via Salnitro

Via Gradaro

Pza Romolo Quazza

V. Pitta Pula

Via Santa

PORTO CATENA

I

Piazzale di Porta Cerese

Vle Salvador Al

Maestto

Marta

(left and below)
Details from Pisanello's cycle: five knights and the death of a knight.

Detail of a sinopia of Pisanello.

ing a partial collapse of the ceiling in what was known as the "Sala del Pisanello" corroborate this. However, the frescoes themselves had completely disappeared until 1969 when Professor Giovanni Paccagnini, then Curator of the museum, after years of dedicated study and courageous research, discovered them under two layers of plaster dating from different periods.

Pisanello's incomplete masterpiece can probably be dated between 1440 and 1444. It illustrates scenes from the chivalric romances of Brittany of which the Gonzaga library had a particularly rich collection. The narrative spills over the walls without interruption or conclusion: knight errants in search of the Holy Grail lost in a hilly, arid landscape with crenellated castles, elegantly dressed women with elaborate coiffures are spectators at a tournament as though suspended in a dream world. This cycle of chivalry and courtly love in

its unfinished and fairy-tale beauty seems to point to the end of an era, the end of medieval civilization, making way for the new world of the Renaissance.

Ludovico II was an excellent example of this new Renaissance man. A disciple of Vittorino da Feltre, Ludovico left an indelible mark on Mantua's history thanks to his intelligent policy of change and progress in the administration of his state. A group of writers, artists and philosophers were brought to his court and gave added prestige to this prince who was not only a cultivated and sensitive Humanist, a devoted reader and student of Virgil, but also an enlightened patron of the arts. In 1459 Mantua was host to the Council called by Pope Pius II. The arrival of the Piccolomini Pope with his retinue of cardinals, bishops, clerics, stewards and chamberlains, with their magnificent vestments, brought unprecedented excitement to the lazy rhythm of provincial life.

The Pope remained in Mantua for almost a year. Using the arrival of the Pope as an excuse, Ludovico moved his court to the Castello di San Giorgio and there he remained enjoying the fresh breezes and the clear, clean lakeside air. The restoration of the inside of the castle was entrusted to Luca Fancelli and there are still traces of his work in some of the rooms notwithstanding the numerous later restorations that the castle underwent.

In the summer of 1460 after protracted and laborious negotiations Andrea Mantegna came to the Gonzaga court where he was to remain until his death in 1506. His prodigious artistic activity

The family and the court of Ludovico II Gonzaga, in the fresco by Andrea Mantegna in the Camera degli Sposi.

Detail of Ludovico and a courtier, possibly his brother Alessandro.

never ceased. Unfortunately for the city, the mismanagement of the later Dukes meant that many of his famous works ended up elsewhere: works such as the *Death of the Virgin*, now in the Prado, the *Madonna of Victory*, *Parnassus* and the *Triumph of Virtue*, now in the Louvre and the *Dead Christ*, in the Brera Gallery in Milan. The only work, and what a masterpiece it is, that remains in Mantua is the justly famous Camera degli Sposi situated in the north-east tower of the castle. This room was frescoed by Mantegna between 1465 and 1474. A small room perfectly square in dimension, it is badly lighted by small irregularly placed windows. Mantegna transformed this dark claustrophobic room into a classical open-air loggia, which was divided into sections by painted columns resting on a decorated base that runs around the entire room. A series of painted leather curtains covers the spaces between the columns on the dark walls, but they are thrown back with theatrical effect on the other two walls to reveal dramatically the Gonzaga family as portrayed by Mantegna. The "warts-and-all" portrayal

Detail of the wife of Ludovico, Barbara of Brandenburg with her children Dorotea, Ludovico and, behind his mother, Rodolfo.

(below right)
The scene called The Meeting

Detail of three courtiers.

of the family makes the people both more human and more understandable, while Andrea's genius for atmospheric evocation makes the court seem both elegant and homey at the same time. The Marquis, seated on a simple but handsome chair, holds a letter in his hands and seems to be discussing its contents with the courtier, perhaps his brother Alessandro, who leans deferentially towards him. Seated beside Ludovico is his wife Barbara of Brandenburg, her square solid body encased in magnificent brocade; her stern and austere expression belies her lively intelligence and extreme sensitivity. Barabara is surrounded by some of the members of her numerous family: the pale Dorotea, the delicate young bishop, Ludovico, Gianfrancesco and, standing directly behind his mother, the son Rodolfo who was to die in the battle of Fornovo. In the background, slightly to one side, is the charming face of the Gonzaga daughter-in-law, the Bavarian Margaret Wittelsbach, her blonde hair caught up by ribbons. Courtiers, in the doublet and hose of the period, crowd the steps leading to the dais on which Ludovico is holding court. A court dwarf is seen standing behind her mistress, Barbara.

The other scene, known as *The Meeting*, takes place in the open air with a background of rocks and hills, a landscape that Mantegna saw as vigorous, lively and verdant. The city on the hill, encircled by a medieval wall, is an idealised picture of Rome in which the Coliseum and the pyramid of Caius Cestius are easily recognisable. Marquis Ludovico, in a gesture that is both a parental welcome and a sign of respect, greets his son Francesco. Francesco has just arrived from Rome where he was made a cardinal thanks primarily to the efforts of the Duke of Milan, Francesco Sforza. The newly appointed cardinal, the first Gonzaga to attain this rank, is surrounded by younger members of the family who greet him with genuine affection: the young bishop Ludovico, his brother, and his charming nephew Sigismondo. The clasped hands of the cardinal, the young bishop and Sigismondo are a symbol of the ecclesiastical tradition in the family and a promise of its continuity. Standing beside his grandfather is the future Marquis Francesco, his agile young body and proud demeanor undoubtedly the result of early training in riding and jousting. Ludovico's first born son and immediate successor, Federico I, stands at the right of the scene facing his father; his magnificent doublet is elaborately draped over his shoulder in a pathetic attempt to hide his deformed back. Family retainers are shown holding in check lively hunting dogs, the ferocious mastifs and a splendidly capa-

Detail of Ludovico greeting his son Francesco newly appointed a cardinal.

(left)
Ludovico's grandchildren: Francesco who became the fourth Marquis and Sigismondo who became a cardinal.

(right)
Detail of the left part of The Meeting.

Self-portrait of Andrea Mantegna on the painted column to the right of the door.

(below right)
The Domus Nova, by Luca Fancelli, begun in 1480.

Detail of the trompe-l'œil sky painted on the ceiling of the Camera degli Sposi.

risoned white horse. Andrea Mantegna himself is part of this meeting: looking very carefully at the painted column to the right of the door one can see his self-portrait amidst the floral decoration. The discovery of this, the authentic self-portrait of the master, was made by the Mantuan scholar Rodolfo Signorini who is also the author of a distinguished book on the cycle of the Camera degli Sposi which casts a new light on the figure of Ludovico II and on the entire scene.

In the centre of the ceiling, beautifully decorated with monochrome portraits of Roman Emperors, is a trompe-l'œil circular opening to the sky. Encircling this, is a balustrade around which are winged cherubs, young girls, an African and a blue peacock. Ludovico slept at least once in this room in a huge bed whose splendid canopy was attached to the wall opposite the fireplace; the actual hooks are still visible. The Marquis was one of the many victims of the plague which swept through Italy once again in 1478; he died at his villa in Goito.

His successor, Federico I, reigned for a brief period, only six years. The only building dating from this period is the Domus Nova, the great square palace designed by Luca Fancelli with its enclosed courtyard and large garden facing towards the lower lake. The construction, begun in 1480 alongside the old Bonacolsi palace, was never finished; only three of the projected four wings were completed. The space that had been intended for a courtyard is today the Piazzetta Paradiso. The east wing overlooking the garden was created to house Federico's private apartments. The grandiose façade of this wing, flanked by two towers with open loggias, is called by the art historian Marani, "one of the greatest examples of the art of Fancelli."

Federico's successor, Francesco II, six years after his father's death in 1484, made a most important marriage to the sixteen-year-old Isabella d'Este, to whom he had been engaged since boyhood. The young bride came to live in the Castello di San Giorgio in apartments next to the south-east tower. Shortly after her arrival Isabella ordered a *Studiolo* to be built; this was a small private room of a kind much in demand by Renaissance rulers as a place for study and meditation. Beneath the Studiolo Isabella placed her *Grotta*, a tiny room with a vaulted ceiling whose precious wood work is today in a state of disrepair. There she prepared the cabinets and treasure

The wooden ceiling of the Studiolo of Isabella d'Este.

(right)
The Sala di Troia, by Giulio Romano.

(left)
The "Great Hall" or Scalcheria, frescoed by Lorenzo Leonbruno.

chests that were to house the collection she was to accumulate in the years to come driven by "that insatiable desire to possess antique things," as she herself wrote. With her lively intelligence, genuine interest in things intellectual, excellent taste and aptitude for politics, she was a fascinating woman. Isabella played a significant role in the artistic and political affairs, both locally and throughout Italy, demonstrating a cleverness and a Machiavellian ability to understand the complex political game of the period. She lived through many difficulties: the battle of Fornovo in 1495, the imprisonment of her husband, the enmity of Pope Julius II who held her son hostage for three years in Rome, and the innumerable love affairs of her Don Giovanni husband. Isabella survived all this with dignity and great personal style. She surrounded herself with exquisite things: paintings, furniture, ceramics, sculptures, coins, books and jewels that were, alas, dispersed in the sack of Mantua in 1630 and the sale of the Gonzaga collection. At the death of her husband in 1519 she moved into ground-floor apartments in the Corte Vecchia which were renovated and redecorated for her in 1522. Some of the apartments that once belonged to Isabella can be visited today.

The "Great Hall" or Scalcheria, frescoed with lively hunting scenes and grotesques by Lorenzo Leonbruno, leads into Isabella's most secluded personal apartments: the Studiolo and the Grotta. Here she brought some of her favourite fittings— wooden candelabra, cupboards with beautifully inlaid doors made by the Mola brothers, and the lovely door with medals by Gian Cristoforo Romano. A craftsman known as Master Sebastiano designed the ceilings in both rooms and Tullio Lombardi created the doors of the Studiolo in 1522. The walls were hung with seven stupendous canvases painted between 1497 and 1530 by Mantegna, Perugino, Costa il Vecchio and Correggio which are today in the Louvre. Isabella's extraordinary collection, which contained around 1600 objects including a *Cupid* by Praxiteles and one by Michelangelo, was for the most part displayed in cupboards, cases and niches in the Grotta; some

The Cortile della Cavallerizza.

objects even stood on the decorative wooden cornices. A short dark corridor decorated with Isabella's mottoes and personal symbols led to a secret sun-filled garden with fountains playing, a spot so delightful that Alberto Cavriani wrote in a letter to Isabella "... and your little garden so green and beautiful that it seems a veritable paradise, those tiny apple trees that bear such enormous fruit, the ripening figs that I so love, the jasmine that reaches to the sky... everything, everything is an invitation to happiness."

In October 1531 Federico II, Isabella's son, proud of his newly obtained title of Duke and determined to carry on the dynasty, decided to take a wife. The main attraction of the bride-to-be, Margherita Paleologo, was her dowry: Monferrato (a vast territory in what is now Piedmont). Giulio Romano, the court architect, was commissioned to decorate two new apartments in the castle and to construct, on the far side of the moat, the so-called Palazzina della Paleologa, which was demolished at the end of the last century. In the years immediately following his marriage, the young Duke decided that he could not renovate the fortress to his satisfaction. The prestige he enjoyed, his reputation in other European courts and his ever increasing desire for splendour led him to order Giulio Romano to create larger, newer living quarters south-east of the castle, the beginning of the Gonzaga's Corte Nuova. The Appartamenti di Troia, designed by Giulio and decorated by his pupils from the master's cartoons, were completed between 1536 and 1539. Erotic themes, such as those used in the Palazzo Te, were discarded as the Duke preferred to dedicate his new palace to the "celebration of the manly arts of war and hunting and to the glorification of the Caesars and the warriors of the Renaissance." The decorations of these rooms became carved or painted frames and works of art were placed in them. In the Saletta dei Cesari, there were Titian's eleven portraits of Roman Emperors (sold to the King of England in 1627 and later sold to Spain where they were destroyed in the 18th century by a fire); the small scenes below (one today is in the Louvre, three at Hampton Court); in the Camerino dei Falconi, the twelve paintings of falcons by Rinaldo Mantovano: in

44

The great reception room, the Sala di Manto.

the Sala di Giove, the busts of great Renaissance condottieri by Alfonso Cittadella; in the Sala dei Cavalli, the nine canvases of different breeds of horses raised by the Gonzaga. A small loggia flanked by the Camerino degli Uccelli and the Camerino dei Falconi leads to the small hanging garden, called the Cortile dei Cani.

Giulio completed the apartments with two of his most brilliant achievements, the Sala di Troia, which illustrates scenes from the Trojan War, and the elegant Loggia dei Mesi, which opens into the Cortile della Cavallerizza (1538-1539). Across from the Loggia Giulio built, around 1539, the Palazzina della Rustica, a two-storey building made entirely of rusticated stone with elaborately carved twisted columns set in the piano nobile, or first floor. The façade of the Rustica is today one of the sides of that unusual courtyard, the Cortile della Cavallerizza, formed by four façades in rusticated stone, three of which are the work of Giulio's successor, Giovan Battista Bertani.

The death of Federico II in June 1540 marked the end of a particularly glorious period of Man-tuan Renaissance and the beginning of the long and wise regency of Cardinal Ercole, brother of the dead Duke. Federico's young son and successor, Francesco III, died of pneumonia at only seventeen, after having fallen into the lake in winter. Of the remaining sons the most interesting and attractive was surely the third-born, Ludovico, but Guglielmo, the second-born, insisted on his rights and, notwithstanding his delicate health and the family infirmity of a hunchback, came to power in 1550. Ludovico played an important part in the family history nonetheless. He went to France to claim the inheritance of his maternal grandmother, Anne d'Alençon, and there he married the Princess of Cleves and founded the branch of the family known as the Gonzaga Nevers, who proved so disastrous when it at last became their turn to rule Mantua.

Guglielmo was a miser and a bigot, of limited intelligence and a provincial snob. He spent his reign accumulating money and trying unsuccessfully to curb the prodigality of his son Vincenzo. Giovan Battista Bertani, his court architect, began an ambitious project for the enlargement of Giulio Romano's Corte Nuova; the project was started

The church of Santa Barbara, built by Giovan Battista Bertani.

(below right)
The Salone dei Fiumi with Baroque frescoes by Giorgio Anselmi.

A room in the Appartamento degli Arazzi, with tapestries woven in Brussels from cartoons by Raphael.

in 1549 but work dragged on until the very end of the century. The basic part of the building erected by Bertani on three sides of the Cortile dei Cani housed the three famous rooms called Sala dei Capitani, Sala dei Marchesi and Sala dei Duchi. The colossal Sala di Manto, dedicated to the soothsayer, the legendary founder of Mantua, became the great reception room. With the construction of the staircase called the Scalone di Enea, Bertani linked the fortress to the palace and created an ante-room, which led to both buildings.

Meanwhile the family church of the city's rulers was built, the church of Santa Barbara. Traces of Bertani's Roman period can be found in the structure of the façade with its airy loggia and massive bell-tower whose marble decoration accentuates the rosy colour of the bricks.

In 1565 Duke Guglielmo decided to give the sumptuous rooms in the Corte Nuova to his three-year-old son Vincenzo and to move to the Corte Vecchia. Here he ordered a radical transformation of the existing medieval building. Today one can identify only a few of Guglielmo's rooms as most of them were re-decorated first by Viani and later by Paolo Pozzo, in the neoclassical style at the end of the 18th century, who transformed them into the Appartamento degli Arazzi. The delicate but over-abundant 18th-century decorations create a framework for the tapestries, woven in Brussels around 1530 from cartoons by Raphael which were bought by Cardinal Ercole. The nine tapestries tell stories of the lives of Saint Peter and Saint Paul as related in the Acts of the Apostles. The most important set of these tapestries is in the Vatican Museum, while the seven extant cartoons are at the Victoria and Albert Museum in London. The Sala dello Zodiaco was only partially restored and there is still a fascinating late-16th-century planetarium, done by Lorenzo Costa il Giovane, frescoed on the ceiling. The court dining room, now the Salone dei Fiumi, was transformed by the Baroque frescoes of Giorgio Anselmi into a trompe-l'œil garden house with allegorical paintings of the rivers in Mantuan territory. This room opens onto the enchanting hanging garden, surrounded by a classical colonnade, the work of Bertani's assistant Pompeo Pedemonte (1579). The 16th-century grotto and fountain were demolished and replaced by the Padiglioncino dei Rinfreschi by Antonio Galli Bibiena, which was built in the later part of the 18th century. The Saletta dei Falconi has frescoes of chubby putti training

hunting falcons in a composition with strong traces of Correggio's influence. Tiny and intimate, the Salottino dei Mori with its Venetian wooden ceiling was probably used by Guglielmo as a *Stufetta* or winter sitting room.

Vincenzo I succeeded his father Guglielmo in 1587 and with him came the last splendid phase of Mantuan art. The architect and painter Anton Maria Viani began yet another transformation and enlargement of the palace on the instructions of the sybaritic Duke Vincenzo. Viani re-decorated existing apartments, created corridors, galleries and passageways, often destroying existing architectural masterpieces. Between 1601 and 1605 Viani completed his most ambitious work, the private apartment of Vincenzo with its long and opulent gallery, the Galleria degli Specchi, to which neoclassical decorations and precious mirrors were added around the end of the 18th century. Here Claudio Monteverdi conducted his newly written music under the smiling gaze of robust young goddesses frescoed on the ceiling.

Next to this gallery is the Salone degli Arcieri, the ante-room reserved for the Duke's special troops with its amusing decoration of yellowish curtains raised to reveal only parts of horses and never the whole animal. Off this hall are three small rooms with elaborate wooden ceilings, decorated with gilded symbolic labyrinths and the

motto of Vincenzo I, "*Forse che sì, forse che no*" (Maybe yes, maybe no). Other smaller rooms, re-done in neoclassical style, and a stairway of red Verona marble lead to the Appartamenti del Paradiso, decorated by Viani for Vincenzo's wife Eleonora dei Medici in Fancelli's 15th-century Domus Nova. These rooms were of a far more manageable size, more practical for day to day living. They seem ideally suited to the solitary, aristocratic woman who lived here: maps and plans of other cities adorn the walls, the small cozy sitting room decorated with storks (supposedly good omens), and the position looking out onto the large garden with the lethargic lower lake in the background.

Meanwhile Viani created for Vincenzo I the regal gallery, the Galleria della Mostra, along the west side of the Cortile della Cavallerizza. The Antiquarium held the most precious part of the Duke's collection of paintings, sculpture and *objets d'art*, works chosen by Vincenzo and displayed here in the three rows of niches of different sizes and depths that Viani had made especially for the collection. Viani's work in the Corte Nuova is evident also in the Galleria delle Metamorfosi which was finished around 1616 and was designed to house the Gonzaga's Museum of Natural History. This room was decorated with frescoes from Ovid's *Metamorphoses*.

According to documents found in the Gonzaga archives, the family also kept in this museum the mummified corpse of Rinaldo Bonacolsi, il Passerino. This macabre souvenir was thought to be a symbol of good luck and its destruction by the last Duchess was believed by many people to be the cause of the family's downfall.

Before the final catastrophe in 1630, Viani planned and executed a strange and mysterious apartment in miniature. These rooms were arbitrarily given the name of Appartamento dei Nani (Apartment of the Dwarfs). It seems more likely that these tiny rooms, which contain a chapel as well as living quarters, were simply further proof of Vincenzo's exhibitionism rather than an actual apartment intended for the court dwarfs. Vincenzo was at this stage a man who had seen and possessed everything and was constantly seeking new and bizarre ways to relieve his boredom.

The Gonzaga palace, after nearly two centuries of neglect, has in recent years undergone a series of intelligent and well-planned renovations which have almost completely restored the entire complex. The Museum in the Corte Nuova houses a collection of Greek and Roman statues from the Gonzaga collection. In the Corte Vecchia besides the coats-of-arms, sculpture, armour and furniture from many different periods are paintings by: Morone, Bonsignori, Francia, Mazzola, Bedoli,

Peter Paul Rubens: The Gongaza Family in Adoration of the Trinity.

(left)
A room in the Appartamento dei Nani.

Rubens (*The Gonzaga Family in Adoration of the Trinity*), Tintoretto, Fetti, Strozzi, Peranda, Torbido, Sustermans, Viani, Bazzani, etc. Many of these paintings have been brought to the palace from churches and monasteries suppressed by the Austrians and others have come from various private collections.

Palazzo Te

Palazzo Te.

Mantua, after Pitentino changed the course of the river in the 12th century, developed as two large islands surrounded by lakes and separated by a canal called "il Rio". There was, however, a third and smaller island whose 14th-century name Tejeto was shortened in the following century to Te. This small island was dismal, swampy and unhealthy until the Gonzaga had it drained and turned it into a place for relaxation and pleasure. Ludovico II used it as a stud farm for developing a highly prized breed of horses and Isabella d'Este wrote that she wished "to place some live hares on the Te, a place encompassed by water yet close on the gates of Mantua, where we can go to enjoy ourselves." Her son, the adored Federico, grew up in a rarefied society of elegant women, a society guided by the taste and intelligence of his mother. Federico's natural amatory inclinations and sensuality were continually being tested by the exciting proximity of his mother's ladies-in-waiting. Charming, lively, audacious girls with names such as: Tortorina, Chiarina, Diana "più

him the unconditional support of the Duke. In 1525 Giulio began work on the construction and decoration of the Palazzo Te. Frequent interruptions held up the work and it was not completely finished until 1535.

Giulio built into the palace pre-existing structures and paid particular attention to the environment so that the palace would blend well into its surroundings. The rooms branch off a central courtyard that at one time contained a box-hedge labyrinth. The original model of this labyrinth, known to us through contemporary drawings, was a similar motif in the palace of the Roman Emperor Domitian. A heraldic symbol is repeated again and again in the rooms of the palace: Mount Olympus rising from the water and surrounded by a labyrinth. The labyrinth in the garden, as well as the rooms that surround it, should be viewed in relation to this symbol.

A large garden at the back (which leads to an 18th-century garden house or esedra) is connected to the palace by a bridge that spans two ponds, at one time filled with water; another repetition of the concept of Mount Olympus rising from the water and surrounded by a labyrinth.

The application of Humanist philosophy and ideals did much to create a non-Christian, almost pagan, atmosphere in Federico's court. Giovio or Equicola, who were prominent members of the Gonzaga academy, were probably responsible for the large number of symbols and allegories used in the decoration of the palace. Certainly it was an atmosphere well suited to Federico's hedonism.

Giulio's bizarre and indefatigable imagination (plus a numerous work force to carry out his ideas), created the ideal setting for the feasts and revels of this Renaissance lord.

The magnificent Sala dei Cavalli, intended as a reception and ballroom, is in fact dedicated to the thoroughbreds so admired by the young Marquis. Federico's favourite horses are portrayed here with extraordinary realism. Authentic portraits of champion stallions whose names were written in large capital letters on the painted architecture that served as frames for the portraits. Late 16th-century documents have provided information about these favourite horses: the superb arab stallion on the south wall to the left of the large fireplace is Morel Favorito; on the west wall the dapple horse with the grey mane is called Glorioso; on the north wall, where the windows face the city, is the noble sorel with a reddish mane named Bataglia (his name reflecting his fiery temperament); on the same wall towards the right the dapple grey whose small proud head is decorated with elegant plumes is Dario.

The magnificent ceiling uses yet again the Mount

calda del sole" (hotter than the sun), Delia, Livia, Paulina, the licentious Brognina and Isabella Balarina who wrote him provocative letters to which he replied with passionate phrases of galantry. When he became Marquis of Mantua he wished, according to Vasari, "to be able to retire to dine far from the formality of the court," remembering no doubt the elegant villas of Rome where he had lived for several years at the court of Pope Julius II. No one was more qualified to interpret his wishes than Giulio Romano who had had previous experience in Rome where he had decorated Villa Madama and the Farnesina. The charming little island with its luxuriant vegetation, secluded by encircling waters, was the ideal place to build a romantic pleasure dome for Federico and his lovely mistress, Isabella Boschetto, Countess of Calvisano and the niece of Baldassarre Castiglione.

As soon as Giulio arrived in Mantua in 1524 he began work on the restoration of the villa at Marmirolo: the excellent results of this work won

(left)
The courtyard façade and the garden house of Palazzo Te.

Detail from the scene of the wedding banquet of Cupid and Psyche in the Sala di Psiche.

Detail of two horses in the Sala dei Cavalli: right, Morel Favorito.

Detail of a salamander with the motto
Quod huic deest me torquet
(What he lacks is that which tortures me).

(left)
Two hunting scenes from the Sala dello Zodiaco.

(left)
The Loggia d'Onore with frescoes from the stories of David.

Federico's bedroom called the Sala delle Aquile.

Olympus motif and here, too, is the salamander, personal symbol of Federico with his motto *Quod huic deest me torquet* (What he lacks is that which tortures me). Federico liked to contrast his warm sensual nature to that of the salamander, which was said to be impervious to fire and insensitive to love. Paolo Giovio wrote: "This lizard has many distinguishing qualities, above all it has the rare gift, unique among all living things, that it never feels love as do all other animals. Federico, Lord of Mantua, has chosen the salamander as his symbol with the motto QUOD HUIC DEEST ME TORQUET. For it was the love of his mistress that tormented him, that love that the salamander knows not."

The symbol is repeated in the Sala di Psiche, a room reserved for the Lord of Mantua's banquets and dedicated to the love affair of Federico and Isabella Boschetto. Here are the voluptuous illustrations of the story of Psyche as told by Apuleius in the *Golden Ass*. The frescoes in this room are highlighted by the lavish decorations of leather, with designs worked with gold and silver, that cover the lower part of the walls. The most valuable marble was used to build the fireplaces and the doors made of semi-precious stones, bronze and inlaid wood—today either lost or destroyed—completed the sumptuous decoration of the room.

Giulio's inexhaustible imagination (he drew the cartoons for all the decorations in the palace) can be seen again in the delicate Sala dello Zodiaco, in which one finds the stucco plaques with the signs of the zodiac and sixteen different medals. The art historian Gombrich has found that these medals illustrate horoscopes in general, without any specific reference to historical figures.

This room leads into the lovely Sala delle Aquile, Federico's bedroom, where the curved ceiling with its elegant stucco decoration and its frescoed pagan myths gives a suggestion of a canopy over the great bed.

The airy Loggia d'Onore, which opens onto the garden and the ponds, connects the palace to the east wing; it is a spectacular open-air reception room with its elaborately decorated vaulted ceiling, a natural frame for the biblical stories of David.

The iconography in the decoration of the rooms in this wing is designed to exalt the power and position of the Emperor Charles V; there are Roman stories and Greek myths in which the figure of Jove resembles the Emperor. These frescoes have a strong political meaning, in fact Charles V was to prove a friend and ally of Federico's.

The delicate ribbing of the painted cupola in the centre of the Sala dei Giganti, enlivened by

Detail of the stucco frieze in the Saletta degli Stucchi.

(right)
Detail of central part of ceiling in the Sala dei Giganti.

The Fall of the Titans, (detail), in the Sala dei Giganti.

a kaleidoscopic effect created by its many geometrical divisions, adds to the startling quality of the room, one of Giulio's masterpieces. The subject here, too, is mythological: Jove's revenge on the giants who had dared to conspire against him. The figure of Jove, seated in solitary splendour under the eagle, dominates the entire scene; around him, in the clouds of Olympus, are the ancient gods. Below this charmed circle are the twisted, tortured figures of the Titans trying in vain to escape destruction. The whole effect is both tragic and grotesque. This wild scene is accentuated by the strange echoes in the room. Giulio created this weird play of sound by a careful study of acoustics; one can almost hear the lament of the Titans and the roar of the stones that are crushing them. The whole scene was also illuminated by the light from a huge fireplace—

which no longer exists—that, as Vasari wrote, created the impression that the Titans were burning.

The stucco frieze in the Saletta degli Stucchi, a masterpiece by Francesco Primaticcio, and the decoration in the Saletta di Cesare, are also clearly intended to exalt and flatter Charles V, from whom Federico obtained the title of Duke in 1530.

Around 1530 the Appartamento della Grotta was built in the north-east corner of the garden: secluded rooms with a small loggia decorated with grotesques and a tiny secret garden. At the bottom of the garden is a grotto used as a bathing place. The entrance is not an elegant threshold or a marble door, but a huge misshapen mass of stone which gives the idea of a natural cavern. This impression was re-inforced inside by the light plaster covering in which sea shells were placed (the shells are no longer there), whose mother-of-pearl surfaces gave off an iridescent light.

Giulio's freedom of interpretation of classical models and of those laid down by other artists, including his master, Raphael, allowed him to create an architecture of a dynamic strength and of a freedom of expression unprecedented in the first decades of the 16th century (Hartt).

Although stripped of its furnishings and surrounded by modern buildings which have distorted its relationship to its environment, Federico Gonzaga's pleasure palace has retained throughout the centuries its dramatic beauty and its magnificence.

The Decline

Imperial troops laid siege to Mantua on 18 July 1630. It was a long and terrible war. Hunger and the plague so weakened the city's defenders that they were unable to keep out the enemy and the city fell. The sack that followed the city's surrender was devastating and the plunder from the Palazzo Ducale, the churches and the villas of the rich was enormous. When the Imperial troops finally left Mantua in 1631, they left behind a ruined city stripped of much of her famous beauty. Never again did Mantua regain that elegance, prestige and luxury that it had enjoyed during the golden age of the Gonzaga family.

Carlo I Gonzaga Nevers made a commendable effort to reconstruct his capital and with Carlo II, libertine though he was, there was a certain rebirth of interest in the arts. In contrast to the progressive decline of the reigning family was the rise both political and financial of certain of the city's other families. Tangible proof of these new fortunes can be found in the buildings that sprung up during this period. Palazzo Canossa (1669) was a restoration along 16th-century lines that enlarged an already existing palace; Palazzo Valenti, probably the work of the Flemish artist F. Geffels; Palazzo Sordi (1660) by F. Geffels with Baroque stucco work inside and with a theatrical, imaginatively conceived courtyard filled with lively decoration.

Worn out by dissipation Carlo II died at only thirty-six years of age, leaving his thirteen-year-old son in the custody of his widow Isabella Clara of Austria. In the portrait of him by an unknown 17th-century artist, the new Duke Ferdinando Carlo appears a self-satisfied, decadent young man, his flaccid face under his curled wig, his glassy eyes, the weak Hapsburg mouth with its slack, slightly opened lips and his ambiguous and vacuous expression.

Following in the steps of his Gonzaga Nevers predecessors, Ferdinando Carlo indulged himself in countless banquets, fêtes and theatrical displays without paying any attention to re-building his dukedom. Politically inept, he allied himself with the French during the War of the Spanish Succession. The war was a defeat for the French and a disaster for Ferdinando Carlo. Fearing Imperial punishment for his part in the war, the Duke fled Mantua in 1707 and sought safety as an exile in Venice. He took with him paintings, pieces of furniture and jewels, as well as a huge amount of gold and silver objects including even his personal chamber-pots made of massive silver and encased in crimson damask. He died in exile in 1708 and, because he had been declared a felon, all rights to the duchy of Mantua passed into the hands of Austria. There were many would-be

(right)
The dome of Sant'Andrea, work of Filippo Juvara.

(far right)
The façade of the Cathedral, by Nicola Baschiera.

Portrait of Ferdinando Carlo, by an unknown 17th-century painter, in the Palazzo D'Arco.

heirs, including a rather large number of illegitimate children, so a bitter law suit developed. The case was argued in the Court of Venice and was at last decided in favour of the Duke of Lorraine who was related to the Gonzaga family through his mother.

The fabulous collection, famous throughout Europe, was dispersed; the immense palaces were stripped and the stables were emptied. This was the tragic end of the once brilliant reign of the Gonzaga. The long period of Austrian domination had begun.

Maria Theresa
and Mantua

The first phase of Austrian rule, between 1707 and 1797, was full of initiative and new civic and private buildings appeared. Some of the signs of the indignities to which the city had been subjected disappeared. In 1716 the reconstruction of the church of San Barnaba was begun by the architect Doricillo Battaglia Moscatelli. The problem of the dome of Sant'Andrea was resolved by the masterful help of Filippo Juvara, who worked on the project around the middle of the century. The Gothic façade of the Cathedral, designed by Dalle Masegne, had so badly deteriorated that, by 1755, a renovation was imperative. It was decided to build a new façade and a contest was held to determine who should be responsible for the construction. The contest was won by Nicola Baschiera, a military engineer then living in Mantua. A direct adaptation from ancient Roman models, Baschiera's project for the Cathedral was rhetorical and in strident contrast with the medieval austerity of the existing buildings in the square.

Building of new palaces continued and among them one must mention: Palazzo Cavriani (1756) and Palazzo degli Studi (1763), both the work of the Bolognese architect Alfonso Torregiani. Between 1756 and 1786 Palazzo Bianchi, today Palazzo Vescovile, was built. This elegant palace, with its impressive row of statues at the top of the building, looks out onto the Piazza Sordello.

The Empress Maria Theresa was an active patron of the arts and under her impetus the "Regia Accademia di Scienze, Lettere e Arti" was created. Between 1767 and 1769 a lovely little theatre was built in the building which housed the Accademia. Designed by Antonio Bibiena, this is a splendid

Interior of the Teatro Scientifico.

The Palazzo Bianchi, today the Bishop's Palace.

example of late-Baroque architecture. Shortly afterwards Giuseppe Piermarini presented a project for a complete reconstruction of the Palazzo dell'Accademia (1773-1775), in which Bibiena's Teatro Scientifico was set as a precious centrepiece. The majestic Palazzo d'Arco was renovated by Antonio Colonna in 1783; it now houses an interesting museum which will shortly be opened to the public.

This fruitful period in Mantua's history ended brusquely when Napoleon's troops marched into the city in 1797. New taxes and heavy fines were imposed on the citizenry and a systematic plunder of all buildings, religious, civic or private began. Andrea Mantegna's *Madonna of Victory*, which had been in the church of Santa Barbara since 1496, was taken to France along with other precious paintings, manuscripts and *objets d'art*.

On 20 February 1810 Andreas Hofer, the leader of the Tyrolean uprising against Napoleon, was executed by a firing squad in a field near Porta Maggiore, one of the city gates. At first the patriot's body was buried in a small garden leading out onto the Piazza Giulia; it was later taken to Innsbruck. There is a commemorative monument on the spot where Hofer was first buried.

The fall of Napoleon brought Mantua back under Austrian domination and a new period of bloody repression. Accused of conspiring against Austria, the "Eleven Martyrs of Belfiore" were first imprisoned in the Castello di San Giorgio and the Mainolda and then executed. These executions took place between 1851 and 1855. Many of the sentences were carried out in the Valletta di Belfiore, at the gates of Mantua, a lovely green field that slopes towards the upper lake. In this section of the lake lotus flowers have sprung up and the great leaves and beautiful flowers are a delight to see during the month of August. The only building of note during this melancholy period in the city's history is the Teatro Sociale (1818-1822), by Luigi Canonica. This unhappy chapter ended in 1866 when Mantua was annexed to the newly formed kingdom of Italy.

The façade of the Teatro Sociale, by Luigi Canonica.

(above)
The battle of the Favorita (1797), a contemporary print.

The Palazzo D'Arco, renovated by Antonio Colonna in 1783.